QUICK LANGUAGES

MULTI-LANGUAGE PHRASEBOOK COLLECTION

AMERICAN
BOOK GROUP

ENGLISH-FRENCH
FRENCH-ENGLISH

QUICK LANGUAGES

MULTI-LANGUAGE PHRASEBOOK COLLECTION

SPEAK ANY LANGUAGE NOW!

WHAT IS QUICK LANGUAGES?

Did you know that we only use about 1,000 words in our everyday vocabulary? The same goes for any language! So, mastering a digital phrasebook with interactive pronunciation tools is a smart alternative to long and expensive language instruction.

Quick Languages is an interactive phrasebook that introduces you to the 12 predominant world languages all in one convenient drop-down menu. Designed for visual, auditory, and kinesthetic learners alike, it is simple, affordable, and effective.

Own the potential of connecting with over 3 billion people!

GET THE AUDIOVISUAL AND INTERACTIVE CONTENT AT QuickLanguages.com

QUICK LANGUAGES

MULTI-LANGUAGE PHRASEBOOK COLLECTION

SPEAK ANY LANGUAGE NOW!

QUICK LANGUAGES PHRASEBOOK COLLECTION
AVAILABLE TITLES

1. ENGLISH-SPANISH & SPANISH-ENGLISH
2. ENGLISH-ITALIAN & ITALIAN-ENGLISH
3. ENGLISH-FRENCH & FRENCH-ENGLISH
4. ENGLISH-GERMAN & GERMAN-ENGLISH
5. ENGLISH-PORTUGUESE & PORTUGUESE-ENGLISH
6. ENGLISH-CHINESE & CHINESE-ENGLISH
7. ENGLISH-ARABIC & ARABIC-ENGLISH
8. ENGLISH-JAPANESE & JAPANESE-ENGLISH
9. ENGLISH-KOREAN & KOREAN-ENGLISH
10. ENGLISH-RUSSIAN & RUSSIAN-ENGLISH
11. ENGLISH-TURKISH & TURKISH-ENGLISH

GET THE AUDIOVISUAL AND INTERACTIVE CONTENT AT QuickLanguages.com

AMERICAN
BOOK GROUP

COMPANION ONLINE COURSE
quicklanguages.com

Quick Languages: 1,000 Key Words and Expressions Phrasebook
ENGLISH-FRENCH & FRENCH-ENGLISH

Author's Copyright © 2023 Quick Languages
Publisher's Copyright © 2023 AMERICAN BOOK GROUP

To request permissions, contact the publisher at info@trialtea.com

Paperback ISBN: 978-1-681655-91-8

Library of Congress Control Code: 2023932191

First paperback edition: April 2023

Edited by Gregorio García
Cover art by Natalia Urbano
Layout by Esmeralda Riveros & Pancho Guijarro

Printed in the USA

American Book Group
americanbookgroup.com

INDEX OF CONTENTS

1,000 KEY WORDS AND EXPRESSIONS

English / French - French / English

Keep practicing at:
QuickLanguages.com

1. Greetings
/ Les Salutations

Hi! / Hello!	**Salut!**
Good morning	**Bonjour**
Good afternoon	**Bonjour**
Good evening / Good night	**Bonsoir/Bonne nuit**
How are you doing?	**Ça va?**
Fine	**Bien**
Very well	**Très bien**
Thank you / Thanks	**Merci**
Thank you very much	**Merci beaucoup**
You're welcome	**Pas de quoi**
Fine, thank you	**Bien, merci**
And you?	**Et toi?**
See you	**A bientôt!**
See you later	**A plus tard!**
See you tomorrow	**A demain!**
Goodbye	**Au revoir!**
Bye	**A plus!**

2. Introductions and Courtesy Expressions / **Les Présentations et Expressions de Politesse**

What is your name?	**Comment vous appelez-vous?**
My name is …	**Je m'appelle…**
Who are you?	**Qui êtes-vous?**
I am …	**Je suis…**
Who is he / she?	**Qui est-il? / Qui est-elle?**
He is … / She is …	**Il est …/ Elle est…**
Nice to meet you / Pleased to meet you	**Enchanté**
Nice to meet you, too	**Moi aussi / Également**
It's my pleasure	**C'est un plaisir**
Excuse me	**Excusez-moi**
Please	**S'il vous plaît**
One moment, please	**Un instant, s'il vous plaît**
Welcome	**Bienvenue**
Go ahead	**Entrez, s'il vous plaît**
Can you repeat, please?	**Pourriez-vous répéter, s'il vous plaît?**
I don't understand	**Je ne comprends pas.**
I understand a little	**Je comprends un petit peu.**
Can you speak more slowly, please?	**Pourriez-vous parler un peu plus lentement, s'il vous plaît?**
Do you speak Spanish?	**Parlez-vous espagnol?**
How do you say hello in Spanish?	**Comment dit-on "salut" en espagnol?**
What does it mean?	**Qu'est-ce que ça veut dire?**
I speak Spanish a little	**Je parle un peu espagnol**

3. Ways to Address a Person
/ Formes de Désignation de la Personne

Madam / Ma'am	**Madame**
Miss	**Mademoiselle**
Ms.	**Mlle**
Mr.	**M**
Mrs.	**Mme**
Sir	**Monsieur**
Dr.	**Docteur**

4. The Articles
/ Les Articles

The	**Le / la / les**
The car	**La voiture**
The cars	**Les voitures**
The house	**La maison**
The houses	**Les maisons**
A	**Un / une**
A car	**Une voiture**
A house	**Une maison**
An	**Un / une**
An elephant	**Un éléphant**
An apple	**Une pomme**
Some	**Des**
Some cars	**Des voitures**
Some houses	**Des maisons**

5. The Subject Pronouns
/ Les Pronoms Personnels

I	**Je**
You	**Tu**
He	**Il / On**
She	**Elle**
It	**Ø**
We	**Nous**
You	**Vous**
They	**Ils**

6. The Possessive Adjectives
/ Les Adjectifs Possessifs

My	**Mon**
Your	**Ton**
His	**Son**
Her	**Sa**
Its	**Son**
Our	**Notre**
Your	**Votre**
Their	**Leur**
My car	**Ma voiture**
Your book	**Ton livre**
His TV	**Son téléviseur**
Our house	**Notre maison**

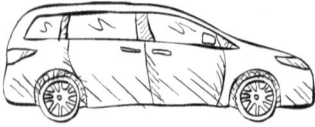

7. The Demonstrative Adjectives / **Les Adjectifs Démonstratifs**

This	**Ce / Cette**
This book	**Ce livre**
This shirt	**Cette chemise**
These	**Ces**
These books	**Ces livres**
These shirts	**Ces chemises**
That	**Ce / cette**
That table	**Cette table**
That car	**Cette voiture**
Those	**Ces**
Those tables	**Ces tables**
Those cars	**Ces voitures**

8. The Possessive Pronouns / **Les Pronoms Possessifs**

Mine	**Le mien**
Yours	**Le tien**
His	**Le sien**
Hers	**La sienne**
Its	**Le sien**
Ours	**Le nôtre**
Yours	**Le vôtre**
Theirs	**Le leur**
The car is mine	**La voiture est à moi**
The book is yours	**Le livre est à toi**
That TV is his	**Le téléviseur est à lui**
This house is ours	**Cette maison est à nous**

9. The Cardinal Numbers
/ Les Nombres Cardinaux

0 / Zero	**Zéro**
1 / One	**Un**
2 / Two	**Deux**
3 / Three	**Trois**
4 / Four	**Quatre**
5 / Five	**Cinq**
6 / Six	**Six**
7 / Seven	**Sept**
8 / Eight	**Huit**
9 / Nine	**Neuf**
10 / Ten	**Dix**
11 / Eleven	**Onze**
12 / Twelve	**Douze**
13 / Thirteen	**Treize**
14 / Fourteen	**Quatorze**
15 / Fifteen	**Quinze**
16 / Sixteen	**Seize**
17 / Seventeen	**Dix-sept**
18 / Eighteen	**Dix-huit**
19 / Nineteen	**Dix-neuf**
20 / Twenty	**Vingt**
21 / Twenty-one	**Vingt-et-un**
30 / Thirty	**Trente**
40 / Forty	**Quarante**
50 / Fifty	**Cinquante**
60 / Sixty	**Soixante**

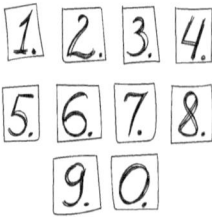

9. The Cardinal Numbers
/ Les Nombres Cardinaux

70 / Seventy	**Soixante-dix**
80 / Eighty	**Quatre-vingt**
90 / Ninety	**Quatre-vingt-dix**
100 / One hundred	**Cent**
101 / One hundred and one	**Cent un**
200 / Two hundred	**Deux cent**
300 / Three hundred	**Trois cent**
400 / Four hundred	**Quatre cent**
500 / Five hundred	**Cinq cent**
600 / Six hundred	**Six cent**
700 / Seven hundred	**Sept cent**
800 / Eight hundred	**Huit cent**
900 / Nine hundred	**Neuf cent**
1,000 / One thousand	**Mille**
10,000 / Ten thousand	**Dix mille**
100,000 / One hundred thousand	**Cent mille**
1,000,000 / One million	**Un million**
1,000,000,000 / One billion	**Un milliard**
Forty-five (45)	**Quarante cinq**
One hundred and twenty-eight (128)	**Cent vingt-huit**
One thousand nine hundred and sixty-three (1,963)	**Mille neuf cent soixante-trois**
Six thousand and thirty-seven (6,037)	**Six mille trente-sept**
Eleven thousand (11,000)	**Onze mille**
Two hundred and seventy-nine thousand (279,000)	**Deux cent soixante-dix-neuf mille**
Two million (2,000,000)	**Deux millions**

10. The Time
/ L'heure

The clock	**L'horloge**
The watch	**La montre**
What time is it?	**Quelle heure est-il?**
It is ...	**Il est...**
It is one o'clock (1:00)	**Il est une heure (1h00)**
It is two o'clock (2:00)	**Il est deux heures (2h00)**
It is three fifteen / It is a quarter past three (3:15)	**Il est trois heures quinze / Il est trois heures et quart (3h15)**
It is four thirty / It is half past four (4:30)	**Il est quatre heures trente / Il est quatre heures et demi (4h30)**
It is five forty-five / It is a quarter to six (5:45)	**Il est cinq heures quarante cinq / Il est six heures moins quart (5h45)**
It is six fifty / It is ten to seven (6:50)	**Il est six heures cinquante / Il est sept heures moins dix (6h50)**
It is noon (12:00 P. M.)	**Il est midi (12h00)**
It is midnight (12:00 A. M.)	**Il est minuit (00h00)**
In the morning	**Le matin**
In the afternoon	**L'après-midi**
In the evening	**Le soir**
At night	**La nuit**
At what time is ...?	**A quelle heure est....?**
At what time is the concert?	**A quelle heure commence le concert?**
At ...	**A...**
At 7:10 P.M. (seven ten in the evening)	**A 7:10 (sept heures dix du soir)**

11. The Days of the Week
/ Les Jours de la Semaine

Monday	**Lundi**
Tuesday	**Mardi**
Wednesday	**Mercredi**
Thursday	**Jeudi**
Friday	**Vendredi**
Saturday	**Samedi**
Sunday	**Dimanche**
What day is today?	**Quel jour sommes-nous?**

12. The Months of the Year
/ Les Mois de l'année

January	**Janvier**
February	**Février**
March	**Mars**
April	**Avril**
May	**Mai**
June	**Juin**
July	**Juillet**
August	**Août**
September	**Septembre**
October	**Octobre**
November	**Novembre**
December	**Décembre**
What is today's date?	**Quelle est la date d'aujourd'hui?**

1,000 Key Words and Phrases

13. The Weather
/ Le Temps

Sunny	**Ensoleillé**
Cloudy	**Nuageux**
Rainy	**Pluvieux**
Humid	**Humide**
Dry	**Sec**
Cold	**Froid**
Warm	**Chaud**
Hot	**Très chaud**
Rain	**Pluie**
Snow	**Neige**
How is the weather today?	**Quel temps fait-il aujourd'hui?**
It's nice	**Il fait beau**
It's sunny	**C'est ensoleillé.**
It's cold in winter	**En hiver il fait froid**
It's raining	**Il pleut**
It's snowing	**Il neige**
I am cold	**J'ai froid**

14. The Seasons
/ Les Saisons

Spring	**Printemps**
Summer	**Été**
Fall	**Automne**
Winter	**Hiver**

15. The Colors
/ Les Couleurs

Yellow	**Jaune**
Red	**Rouge**
Blue	**Bleu**
Green	**Vert**
Orange	**Orange**
Brown	**Marron**
Pink	**Rose**
Purple	**Violet**
Black	**Noir**
White	**Blanc**
Gray	**Gris**
Light	**Clair**
Dark	**Foncé**
Light green	**Vert clair**
Orange book	**Un livre orange**
Brown shoes	**Des chaussures marrons**
My blouse is white	**Ma blouse est blanche**
What color is...?	**De quelle couleur est...?**
What is your favorite color?	**Quelle est ta couleur préférée?**

16. The Parts of the Face
/ Les Parties du Visage(s)

Cheek	**La joue**
Chin	**Le menton**
Ear	**L'oreille**
Eye	**L'œil**
Forehead	**Le front**
Hair	**Les cheveux**
Lips	**Les lèvres**
Mouth	**La bouche**
Nose	**Le nez**
Skin	**La peau**
Teeth	**Les dents**
Tooth	**Le dent**
Blond / Blonde	**Blond / Blonde**
Brown	**Brun**
Gray	**Cheveux gris**
Red hair	**Roux**
Long	**Long**
Short	**Court**
Straight	**Raide**
Curly	**Frisé**
John is blond	**John est blond**
Karen has long hair	**Karen a les cheveux longs**
He has green eyes	**Il a les yeux verts**
Her eyes are blue	**Ses yeux sont bleus**
His eyes are big and brown	**Ses yeux sont grands et marrons**

17. Essential Verbs / Verbes de Base

Be	**Être**
Go	**Aller**
Come	**Venir**
Have	**Avoir**
Get	**Prendre / obtenir**
Help	**Aider**
Love	**Aimer**
Like	**Apprécier**
Want	**Vouloir**
Buy	**Acheter**
Sell	**Vendre**
Read	**Lire**
Write	**Écrire**
Drink	**Boire**
Eat	**Manger**
Open	**Ouvrir**
Close	**Fermer**
Look at	**Regarder**
Look for	**Chercher**
Find	**Trouver**
Start	**Commencer**
Stop	**Arrêter**
Pull	**Tirer**

17. Essential Verbs
/ Verbes de Base

Push	**Pousser**
Send	**Envoyer**
Receive	**Recevoir**
Turn on	**Allumer**
Turn off	**Éteindre**
Listen to	**Écouter**
Speak	**Parler**
Do	**Faire**
Drive	**Conduire**
Feel	**Sentir**
Know	**Savoir**
Leave	**Partir / sortir**
Live	**Vivre**
Make	**Faire, effectuer, fabriquer**
Meet	**Rencontrer**
Need	**Avoir besoin**
Pay	**Payer**
Play	**Jouer**
Remember	**Se rappeler**
Repeat	**Répéter**
Say	**Dire**
Sit	**S'asseoir**
Sleep	**Dormir**

17. Essential Verbs / Verbes de Base

English	French
Study	**Étudier**
Take	**Prendre**
Think	**Penser**
Understand	**Comprendre**
Wait	**Attendre**
Watch	**Regarder**
There is	**Il y a**
There are	**Il y a**
I am tall	**Je suis grand**
You are short	**Tu es petit**
He is thin	**Il est maigre**
We are big	**Nous sommes grands**
They are intelligent	**Ils sont intelligents**
I am at home	**Je suis à la maison**
You are at school	**Tu es à l'école**
We are at the store	**Nous sommes au magasin**
I get a prize	**Je reçois un prix**
I go to the movies	**Je vais au cinéma**
I have a nice car	**J'ai une belle voiture**
I listen to the music	**J'écoute la musique**
I watch TV.	**Je regarde la télévision**
I like this book	**J'aime bien ce livre**
There are ten children in the park	**Il y a dix enfants dans le parc**

18. Interrogative Words
/ Les Adverbes Interrogatifs

How many ...?	**Combien...?**
How much...?	**Combien...?**
How ...?	**Comment...?**
What ...?	**Quoi...?**
When ...?	**Quand...?**
Where ...?	**Où...?**
Which ...?	**Lequel...? / Laquelle...?**
Who ...?	**Qui...?**
Whose ...?	**A qui...?**
Whom ...? / To whom ...?	**A qui...?**
Why ...?	**Pourquoi...?**
Because ...	**Parce que...?**

19. Linking Words
/ Les Conjonctions

And	**Et**
But	**Mais**
Or	**Ou**
Either ... or	**Ou bien ... ou ...**
Neither ... nor	**Ni...ni...**
Yes	**Oui**
No	**Non**
So	**Donc**
While	**Pendant**

20. The Prepositions / Les Prépositions

About	**Concernant**
Above	**Au dessus**
Across	**A travers**
At	**A, sur, vers**
Behind	**Derrière**
Below	**Au dessous**
Between	**Entre**
By	**Par**
Down	**En bas**
During	**Durant**
For	**Pour**
From	**De**
In	**Dans, en**
In front of	**En face / devant**
Into	**En**

20. The Prepositions
/ Les Prépositions

Near	**Près de**
Next to	**A côté**
Of	**De**
On	**Sur / par dessus**
Out	**Dehors**
Over	**Sur**
Per	**Par**
Through	**A travers**
To	**Vers**
Under	**Sous**
Up	**En haut**
With	**Avec**
Without	**Sans**
The cat is in the box	**Le chat est dans la boîte**
The vase is on the table	**Le vase est sur la table**
Somebody is at the door	**Quelqu'un est à la porte**

21. Giving Directions / Les Indications

At the corner	**Au coin**
Far	**Loin**
Near	**Proche**
Go straight ahead	**Continuez tout droit**
Left	**A gauche**
Right	**A droite**
Turn left	**Tournez à gauche**
Turn right	**Tournez à droite**
Go straight one block	**Continuez tout droit, sur un pâte de maison**
After the traffic light, turn right	**Après le feu, tournez à droite**
How can I get to ...?	**Comment puis-j'aller à ...?**
Where is the ...?	**Où se trouve...?**
Where is the church?	**Où se trouve l'église?**
The museum is next to the shopping center	**Le musée se trouve à côté du centre commercial**
The drugstore is in front of the building	**La pharmacie se trouve en face du bâtiment**
The supermarket is near the park	**Le supermarché est près du parc**

22. The Ordinal Numbers
/ Les Nombres Ordinaux

First	**Premier**
Second	**Deuxième**
Third	**Troisième**
Fourth	**Quatrième**
Fifth	**Cinquième**
Sixth	**Sixième**
Seventh	**Septième**
Eighth	**Huitième**
Ninth	**Neuvième**
Tenth	**Dixième**
Eleventh	**Onzième**
Twelfth	**Douzième**
Twentieth	**Vingtième**
Thirtieth	**Trentième**
The first building	**Le premier bâtiment**
The second floor	**Le deuxième étage**

23. Countries, Nationalities, and Languages / **Les Pays, Nationalités, et Langues**

Brazil (Country)	**Le Brésil (Pays)**
Brazilian (Nationality)	**brésilien, brésilienne (Nationalité)**
Portuguese (Language)	**Portugais (Langue)**
Colombia	**La Colombie**
Colombian	**Colombien / Colombienne**
Spanish	**Espagnol**
China	**La Chine**
Chinese	**Chinois / Chinoise**
Chinese	**Chinois**
England	**L'Angleterre**
English	**Anglais / Anglaise**
English	**Anglais**
France	**La France**
French	**Français / Française**
French	**Français**
Germany	**L'Allemagne**
German	**Allemand / Allemande**
German	**Allemand**
Italy	**L'Italie**

23. Countries, Nationalities, and Languages / **Les Pays, Nationalités, et Langues**

Italian	**Italien / Italienne**
Italian	**Italien**
Japan	**Le Japon**
Japanese	**Japonais / Japonaise**
Japanese	**Japonais**
Mexico	**Le Mexique**
Mexican	**Mexicain / Mexicaine**
Spanish	**Espagnol**
Spain	**L'Espagne**
Spanish	**Espagnol / Espagnole**
Spanish	**Espagnol**
United States of America (U.S.A.)	**Les États Unis d'Amérique**
American	**Américain / Américaine**
English	**Anglais**
Where are you from?	**D'où êtes vous?**
I am from Brazil	**Je suis du Brésil**
I am Brazilian	**Je suis brésilien**
I speak Portuguese	**Je parle portugais**
I am not from Italy	**Je ne suis pas d'Italie**

24. Indefinite Pronouns / Les Pronoms Indéfinis

Anybody	Quelqu'un (interrogatif), personne (négatif)
Anything	Quelque chose (interrogatif), rien (négatif)
Nobody	**Personne**
Nothing	**Rien**
Somebody	**Quelqu'un (affirmatif)**
Something	**Quelque chose (affirmatif)**
Everybody	**Tous**
Everything	**Tout**
Is anybody home?	**Y a-t-il quelqu'un dans la maison?**
I don't want anything	**Je ne veux rien**
Nothing happened	**Il ne s'est rien passé**
Somebody is in the living room	**Quelqu'un est dans le salon**
Everything is ready	**Tout est prêt**

25. The Emotions
/ Les Émotions

Angry	**Fâché, furieux**
Bored	**Ennuyeux**
Confident	**Sûr de soi**
Confused	**Confondu**
Embarrassed	**Embarrassé**
Excited	**Enthousiaste**
Happy	**Heureux**
Nervous	**Nerveux**
Proud	**Fier**
Sad	**Triste**
Scared	**Effrayé**
Shy	**Timide**
Surprised	**Surpris**
Worried	**Soucieux**
I am happy	**Je suis heureux**
He is sad	**Il est triste**
They are surprised	**Ils sont surpris**
Are you excited?	**Es-tu enthousiaste?**
I am not bored	**Je ne m'ennuie pas**
She is not nervous	**Elle n'est pas nerveuse**
Everybody is confident	**Ils sont tous sûrs d'eux**

26. Adverbs
/ Les Adverbes

A few	**Quelques**
A little	**Peu**
A lot	**Beaucoup**
After	**Après**
Again	**Encore**
Ago	**Avant**
Also	**Aussi**
Always	**Toujours**
Before	**Il y a**
Enough	**Suffisant**
Everyday	**Chaque jour**
Exactly	**Exactement**
Finally	**En fin de compte / Finalement**
First	**D'abord**
Here	**Ici**
Late	**Tard**
Later	**Plus tard**
Never	**Jamais**
Next	**Suivant**
Now	**Maintenant**

26. Adverbs
/ Les Adverbes

Often	**Souvent**
Once	**Une fois**
Only	**Seulement**
Outside	**Dehors**
Really	**Vraiment**
Right here	**Ici**
Right now	**Tout de suite**
Since	**Depuis**
Slowly	**Lentement**
Sometimes	**Puisque**
Soon	**Bientôt**
Still	**Toujours**
Then	**Plus tard**
There	**Là-bas**
Today	**Aujourd'hui**
Tomorrow	**Demain**
Tonight	**Ce soir**
Too	**Aussi**
Usually	**Habituellement / Normalement**

27. Auxiliary Verbs
/ Autres Verbes

Can	**Pouvoir (possibilité)**
Could	**Pouvoir (amabilité)**
Did	**Être / Avoir (pour la formation des temps composés)**
Do	**Faire**
Does	**Faire**
Have to	**Il faut + infinitif**
May	**Pouvoir (pour demander la permission)**
Must	**Devoir (obligation)**
Should	**Devoir (pour conseiller)**
Will	**(Auxiliare du Temps Futur)**
Would	**(Auxiliare du Conditionel)**
Can you go to the movies?	**Peux-tu venir au cinéma?**
Could I have change?	**Pourrais-je avoir de la monnaie?**
Did you work at the drugstore?	**Tu as travaillé à la pharmacie?**
I did not (didn't) work at the drugstore	**Je n'ai pas travaille à la pharmacie?**
Do you work at the drugstore?	**Est-ce que tu travailles à la pharmacie**
I do not (don't) work at the drugstore	**Je ne travaille pas à la pharmacie**
Does he read the newspaper?	**Est-ce qu'il lit le journal?**
He does not (doesn't) read the newspaper	**Il ne lit pas le journal**
I have to do my homework	**Je dois faire mon devoir**
May I help you?	**Est-ce que je peux t'aider?**
You must turn left now	**Tu dois tourner à gauche**
You should go to the doctor	**Tu devrais aller chez le docteur**
I will work tomorrow	**Demain je travaillerai**
I would like a glass of wine	**J'aimerais un verre de vin**

28. Expressions
/ Des Expressions

All right	**D'accord**
Come in	**Entre / Entrez**
Come here, please	**Venez ici, s'il vous plaît**
Don't worry!	**Ne t'inquiète pas!**
For example	**Par exemple**
Good luck!	**Bon courage!**
Great idea!	**Excellente idée!**
Have a nice day!	**Bonne journée!**
Help yourself!	**Sers-toi!**
Here you are	**S'il vous plaît!**
Hurry up!	**Dépêche-toi!**
I agree	**Je suis d'accord**
I disagree	**Je ne suis pas d'accord**
I don't care	**Ça ne m'intéresse pas**
I don't know	**Je ne sais pas**
I'm coming!	**Je viens**
I'm afraid...	**J'ai bien peur que...**
It's a deal!	**Marché conclu!**
Keep well!	**Prends soin de toi!!**
Let me think	**Laisse-moi réfléchir**
Let's go!	**Allons-y!**
Right now	**Tout de suite!**
Sounds good!	**Ça me paraît bien**
Sure	**Sûrement**
Take a seat	**Assieds-toi / Asseyez-vous!**
Take care!	**Prends soin de toi!**

29. The Family
/ La Famille

Father	**Le père**
Mother	**La mère**
Son	**Le fils**
Daughter	**La fille**
Brother	**Le frère**
Sister	**Le sœur**
Grandfather	**Le grand-père**
Grandmother	**La grand-mère**
Uncle	**L'oncle**
Aunt	**La tante**
Cousin	**Le cousin / la cousine**
Nephew	**Le neveu**
Niece	**La nièce**
Husband	**Le mari**
Wife	**La femme**
Boyfriend	**Le fiancé**
Girlfriend	**La fiancée**
In-laws	**Les beaux-parents**
Father in-law	**Le beau-père**
Mother in-law	**La belle-mère**
Brother in-law	**Le beau-frère**
Sister in-law	**La belle-soeur**
Step father	**Le beau-père**
Step mother	**La belle-mère**
Step brother	**Le demi-frère**
Step sister	**La demi-soeur**
Who is he?	**Qui est-il?**
He is my brother	**C'est mon frère**

30. The House
/ La Maison

English	French
Living room	**Le salon**
Door	**La porte**
Window	**La fenêtre**
Sofa	**Le canapé**
Lamp	**La lampe**
Dining room	**La salle à manger**
Table	**La table**
Chair	**La chaise**
Kitchen	**La cuisine**
Stove	**La cuisinière**
Oven	**Le four**
Fridge	**Le réfrigérateur**
Microwave	**Le four à micro-ondes**
Bedroom	**La chambre à coucher**
Bed	**Le lit**
Nightstand	**La table de nuit**
Vanity	**La coiffeuse**
Chest of drawers	**La commode**
Closet	**Le vestiaire**
Bathroom	**La salle de bain**
Mirror	**Le miroir**
Sink	**Le lavabo**
Toilet	**Les toilettes**
Bathtub	**La baignoire**
Laundry room	**La chambre d'utilité**
Driveway	**Le parking**
Where is the living room?	**Où se trouve le salon?**
The door is big	**La porte est grande**
The stove is small	**La cuisinière est petite**
The kitchen is beautiful	**La cuisine est belle**

31. The City
/ La Ville

Block	Le paté de maison
Building	L'immeuble
Church	L'église
Movie theater	Le cinéma
Museum	Le musée
Park	Le parc
Drugstore	La pharmacie
Restaurant	Le restaurant
Shopping center	Le centre commercial
Store	Le magasin
Street	La rue
Supermarket	Le supermarché

32. At the Supermarket
/ Au Supermarché

The food	**La nourriture**
The fruits	**Les fruits**
Apple	**La pomme**
Banana	**La banane**
Cherry	**La cerise**
Grapes	**Les raisins**
Orange	**L'orange**
Strawberry	**La fraise**
The vegetables	**Les légumes**
Beans	**Les haricots**
Carrot	**La carotte**
Cauliflower	**Le chou-fleur**
Lettuce	**La laitue**
Onion	**L'oignon**
Pepper	**Le poivron**
Potato	**La pomme de terre / la patate**
Tomato	**La tomate**
The meats	**Les viandes**
Beef	**Le boeuf**
Chicken	**Le poulet**
Turkey	**La dinde**
Ham	**Le jambon**
Pork	**Du porc**
The dairy products	**Les produits laitiers**
Butter	**Le beurre**
Cheese	**Le fromage**
Milk	**Le lait**

32. At the Supermarket
/ Au Supermarché

Yogurt	**Le yaourt**
Jam	**La confiture**
Bread	**Le pain**
Eggs	**Les œufs**
Fish	**Le poisson**
Seafood	**Les fruits de mer**
Can	**La conserve**
Cart	**Le caddie**
Bag	**Le sac**
Basket	**Le panier**
Bottle	**La bouteille**
Cash register	**La caisse**
Cashier	**Le caissier / la caissière**
Customer service	**Le service aux clients**
Groceries	**Épicerie**
How many...?	**Combien...?**
How many oranges do you buy?	**Combien d'oranges achetez-vous...?**
How much does it cost?	**Combien coûte ...? / Combien coûtent ... ?**
How much do the bananas cost?	**Combien coûtent les bananes?**
I want...	**Je veux...**
I want to buy a bottle of milk	**Je veux acheter une bouteille de lait**
I would like...	**J'aimerais ...**
I would like a bag of tomatoes	**Je voudrais un sac de tomates**
Where is the lettuce?	**Où sont les laitues?**
It's on aisle one	**Elles sont dans l'allée numéro un**
Where are the cans of vegetables?	**Où se trouvent les conserves de légumes?**
They are on aisle five	**Ils sont dans l'allée numéro cinq**

33. At the Restaurant
/ Au Restaurant

Waiter / waitress	**Le serveur / la serveuse**
Breakfast	**Petit-déjeuner**
Lunch	**Déjeuner**
Dinner	**Dîner**
To eat	**Manger**
To drink	**Boire**
To eat breakfast	**Prendre le petit-déjeuner**
The menu	**Le menu**
Appetizer	**L'entrée**
Salad	**La salade**
Soup	**La soupe**
Main course	**Le repas principal**
Pasta	**Les pates**
Rice	**Le riz**
French fries	**Les frites**
Mashed potatoes	**La purée de pomme de terre**
Baked potatoes	**Patates au four**
Barbecue	**Le barbecue**
Fried chicken	**Du poulet roti**
Steak	**Le bifteck**

33. At the Restaurant
/ Au Restaurant

Dessert	**Le dessert**
Beverages	**Les boissons**
Coffee	**Le café**
Tea	**Le thé**
Soda	**La boisson gazeuse**
Lemonade	**Le limonade**
Orange juice	**Le jus d'orange**
Alcoholic drinks	**Les boissons alcoolisées**
Beer	**La bière**
Wine	**Le vin**
Check	**L'addition**
Tip	**Le pourboire**
How may I help you?	**Que désirez-vous?**
What would you like to order?	**Qu'allez-vous commander?**
May I have the menu, please?	**Le menu, s'il vous plaît!**
Could I get more water, please?	**Pourriez-vous m'apporter encore un peu plus d'eau, s'il vous plaît?**
My order is wrong	**Je n'ai pas commandé ça**
The service here is wonderful!	**Le service est très bon ici**
The food is delicious!	**La nourriture est délicieuse**
The check, please	**L'addition, s'il vous plaît**
The tip is included	**Le pourboire est inclus**

34. The Office
/ Le Bureau

Book	**Le livre**
Calculator	**La calculatrice**
Computer	**L'ordinateur**
Desk	**Le bureau**
Fax machine	**Le fax**
File	**Le fichier**
File cabinet	**Le classeur**
Folder	**La chemise**
Keyboard	**Le clavier**
Monitor	**Le moniteur**
Mouse	**La souris**
Notebook	**L'agenda**
Pad	**Le bloc-notes**
Paper	**Le papier**
Pen	**Le stylo**
Printer	**L'imprimante**
Ruler	**La règle**
Scissors	**Les ciseaux**
Screen	**L'écran**
Stapler	**L'agrafeuse**
Telephone	**Le téléphone**
My computer is broken	**Mon ordinateur est cassé**
There is no paper in the printer	**Il n'y a pas de papier dans l'imprimante**
We need to buy more folders	**Nous devons acheter encore des chemises**
We don't have a copy machine	**Nous n'avons pas de photocopieuse**

35. Jobs and Positions / Les Emplois et Positions

Accountant	**Comptable**
Architect	**Architecte**
Artist	**Artiste**
Chef	**Cuisinier en chef**
Clerk	**Un employé de bureau / une employée de bureau**
Cook	**Cuisinier / cuisinière**
Doctor	**Docteur**
Engineer	**Ingénieur**
Gardener	**Jardinier**
Graphic designer	**Graphiste**
Lawyer	**Avocat**
Nurse	**Infirmier / Infirmière**
Physician	**Médecin**
Salesperson	**Vendeur / Vendeuse**
Secretary	**Secrétaire**
Security guard	**Gardien**
Taxi driver	**Chauffeur de taxi**
Teacher	**Professeur**
Technician	**Technicien**
Tourist guide	**Guide touristique**
Travel agent	**Agent de voyage**

36. Job Interview
/ Entretien Professionnel

Apply for a job	**Postuler pour un poste**
Duty	**En poste**
Experience	**Expérience**
Last name	**Nom de famille**
First name	**Prénom**
Full time job	**Travail à temps plein**
Part time job	**Travail à temps partiel**
Résumé	**Curriculum Vitae**
Skill	**Compétences**
Work	**Travailler / Travail**

37. The Transportation
/ Les Moyens de Transport

Airplane	**L'Avion**
Bicycle	**Le vélo**
Bus	**L'autobus**
Car	**La voiture**
Helicopter	**L' hélicoptère**
Metro	**Le métro**
Motorcycle	**La moto**
Train	**Le train**
Truck	**Le camion**

38. The Traffic / La Circulation

Bus stop	**La station de bus**
Crosswalk	**Le passage piéton**
Freeway, highway	**L'autoroute**
Gas station	**La station d'essence**
Intersection	**Le carrefour**
Lane	**La file**
No outlet	**La rue sans issue**
One way	**La rue à sens unique**
Pedestrian	**Le piéton**
Speed	**La vitesse**
Stop sign	**Le signe "Stop"**
To get in	**Monter / Rentrer dans**
To get off	**Descendre de / Sortir de**
Toll	**Le péage**
Traffic light	**Le feu rouge**
Train station	**La gare ferroviaire**
Two way	**Aller-retour**
U-turn	**Demi-tour**
Yield	**Accorder la priorité à**
I get in the car	**Je rentre dans la voiture**
I get off the car	**Je descends de la voiture**
We wait for the train	**Nous attendons le train**

39. The Car
/ La Voiture

Accelerator	**L'accélérateur**
Battery	**La batterie**
Hood	**Le capot**
Brake	**Le frein**
Clutch	**L'embrayage**
Engine	**Le moteur**
Fender	**L'aile**
Gear box	**La boîte de vitesse**
Headlight	**Les phares**
Rear view mirror	**Le rétroviseur**
Make	**La marque**
Model	**Le model**
Radiator	**Le radiateur**
Steering wheel	**Le volant**
Seat	**Le siège**
Tire	**Le pneu**
Trunk	**Le coffre**
Wheel	**La roue**
Windshield	**Le pare-brise**
Windshield wipers	**Essuie-glace**
The car is broken	**La voiture est en panne**
I have a flat tire	**J'ai une creveson**
I need a new battery	**J'ai besoin d'une nouvelle batterie**
What year is the car?	**De quelle année est la voiture?**
What make is the car?	**Quelle est la marque de la voiture?**
What model is the car?	**Quel est le model de la voiture?**
How many miles does the car have?	**Combien de milles a la voiture?**

40. Phone Conversations / Des Conversations Téléphoniques

Call	**Téléphoner**
Dial	**Composer un numéro**
Directory	**Annuaire téléphonique**
Directory Assistance	**Les renseignements**
Extension	**Numéro interne**
Hold on, please	**Ne raccrochez pas, s'il vous plaît / Un instant s'il vous plaît**
I'd like to speak to...	**J'aimerais parler avec...**
I'll put you through	**Je vous passe...**
I'll transfer your call	**Je vous transfert la conversation**
I'm calling about ...	**Je vous téléphone concernant...**
Just a minute	**Attendez une minute**
Leave a message	**Laisser un message**
Let me see...	**Laissez-moi regarder ....**
Phone	**Téléphoner**
Phone number	**Numéro de téléphone**
Ring	**Sonner**
Speak	**Parler**
Speaking	**Au téléphone**
Take a message	**Transmettre quelque chose**
Talk	**Parler**
This is...	**C'est ... à l'appareil**
Who's calling?	**Qui est à l'appareil?**

41. At the Post Office
/ A la Poste

Air mail	**Par avion**
Counter	**Guichet**
Envelope	**L'enveloppe**
Letter	**La lettre**
Mail	**Le courrier**
Parcel	**Le colis**
Postcard	**La carte postale**
Postman, mailman	**Le facteur**
Stamp	**Le timbre**
To send	**Envoyer**
To deliver	**Livrer**
Delivery	**Livraison**
To pick up	**Prendre**
Address	**Adresse**
I want to send a letter	**Je veux envoyer une lettre**
I would like to pick up a parcel	**Je voudrais prendre un colis**
How much do the stamps cost?	**Quel est le prix des timbres?**
Do you sell postcards?	**Est-ce que vous vendez des cartes postales?**

42. At the Bank / A la Banque

Account	**Le compte**
ATM	**Le distributeur automatique**
Bank statement	**Le relevé banquaire**
Bank teller	**Le caissier / la caissière**
Cash	**L'argent liquide**
Checkbook	**Le chéquier**
Checking account	**Le compte chèque**
Credit card	**La carte de crédit**
Debit card	**La carte de débit**
Deposit slip	**La fiche de dépôt**
Savings account	**Le compte épargne**
To deposit	**Déposer**
To save	**Épargner**
To transfer	**Faire un transfert**
To withdraw	**Retirer / Faire un retrait**
Transactions	**Les transactions**
Withdrawal slip	**Le reçu**
I want to make a deposit	**Je voudrais faire un dépôt**
Do you have a savings account?	**Est-ce que vous avez un compte épargne?**
I have a checking account	**J'ai un compte courant.**
What is your credit card number?	**Quel est le numéro de votre carte de crédit?**
I don't have an ATM card	**Je n'ai pas de carte de retrait.**
Where are the deposit slips?	**Où sont les fiches du dépôt?**

43. At the Airport
/ A l'Aéroport

Arrival	**Arrivée**
Concourse	**La salle d'attente**
Customs	**Les douanes**
Departure	**Départ**
Destination	**Destination**
Entrance	**Entrée**
Exit	**Sortie**
First class	**Première classe**
Flight	**Le vol**
Gate	**La porte**
Immigrations office	**Le service d'immigration**
Luggage	**Les bagages**
Passport	**Le passeport**
Restrooms	**Les toilettes**
Suitcase	**La valise**
To arrive	**Arriver**
To depart	**Partir**
To travel	**Voyager**
Trip	**Voyage**
Where are you traveling?	**Où allez-vous?**
May I have your ticket, please?	**Puis-je voir votre billet, s'il vous plaît?**
I need you passport, please	**Montrez-moi votre passeport, s'il vous plaît**
My flight number is ...	**Le numéro de mon vol est le...**
Where is gate number ...?	**Où est la porte numéro...?**
The flight is delayed	**Le vol est en retard**
The flight is on time	**Le vol est à l'heure**

44. At the Hotel
/ A l'Hôtel

Double room	**La chambre double**
Single room	**La chambre simple**
Bell desk	**Le bureau d'information**
Bellman	**Le porteur**
Elevator	**L' ascenseur**
Reception	**La réception**
Receptionist	**Le/la réceptionniste**
Reservation	**La réservation**
Stairway	**L'escalier**
Swimming pool	**La piscine**
Tours desk	**Le bureau du tourisme**
Valet parking	**Le service de parking**
To check-in	**L'enregistrement**
To check-out	**L'enregistrement**
I would like to make a reservation	**Je voudrais faire une réservation**
I want a single room	**Je voudrais une chambre simple**
I would like to check-in	**Je voudrais m'enregistrer**

45. The Clothes
/ Les Vêtements

Bathing suit	**Le maillot de bain**
Belt	**La ceinture**
Blouse	**La blouse**
Coat	**Le manteau**
Dress	**La robe**
Gloves	**Les gants**
Hat	**Le chapeau**
Jacket	**Le veston**
Pants	**Les pantalons**
Purse	**Le sac**
Scarf	**Le foulard**
Shirt	**La chemise**
Shoes	**Les chaussures**
Shorts	**Un short**
Skirt	**La jupe**
Socks	**Les chaussettes**
Suit	**Le costume**
Suitcase	**La valise**
The size	**La taille**
Small	**Petite**
Medium	**Moyenne**
Large	**Grande**
Big sizes	**Grandes tailles**

46. At the Shopping Center / Au Centre Commercial

Department store	**Département**
Ladies	**Dames**
Men	**Messieurs**
Juniors	**Adolescents**
Kids	**Enfants**
Ladies' department	**Départment des dames**
Jewelry	**La bijouterie**
Fitting room	**La cabine d'essayage**
Elevator	**L'ascenseur**
Escalator	**L'escalator**
How may I help you?	**Puis-je vous aider?**
I'm looking for ...	**Je cherche...**
I'm just looking	**Je ne fais que regarder**
Where is the fitting room?	**Où est la cabine d'essayage?**
It fits well	**Ça me va bien?**
It doesn't fit well	**Ça ne me va pas bien**
May I pay here?	**Est-ce que je peux payer ici?**
I want to exchange this	**Je voudrais changer cela**
I want to return this	**Je voudrais rendre ça**
I like ...	**Ça me plaît**
I like this blouse	**Cette blouse me plaît**
I don't like ...	**Ça ne me plaît pas**
I don't like these pants	**Ce pantalon ne me plaît pas**

47. At the Drugstore
/ A la Pharmacie

Antiseptic	**Le désinfectant**
Adhesive bandage	**L'adhésif**
Antibiotic	**L'antibiotique**
Aspirin	**L'aspirine**
Bandage	**La bande de pansement**
Cold medicine	**Le médicament pour refroidissement**
Cough syrup	**Le sirop pour la toux**
Medication	**Les médicaments**
Ointment	**La pommade**
OTC (Over The Counter) medication	**Les médicaments génériques**
Painkiller	**Le calmant**
Pills	**Les pastilles**
Prescription	**La prescription**
Tablets	**Les tablettes**
Thermometer	**Le thermomètre**
Cotton	**Le coton**

48. The Parts of the Body
/ Les Parties du Corps

Ankle	**La cheville**
Arm	**Le bras**
Back	**Le dos**
Buttock	**Les fesses**
Calf	**Le mollet**
Chest	**La poitrine**
Elbow	**Le coude**
Feet	**Les pieds**
Finger	**Le doigt**
Foot	**Le pied**
Forearm	**L'avant-bras**
Hand	**La main**
Head	**La tête**
Hip	**La hanche**
Knee	**Le genou**
Leg	**La jambe**
Neck	**Le cou**
Shoulder	**L'épaule**
Stomach	**L'estomac**
Thigh	**La cuisse**
Toe	**L'orteil**
Waist	**Le tour de taille**
Wrist	**Le poignet**

49. Health Problems
/ Les Problèmes de Santé

Backache	**Douleurs dans le dos**
Cold	**Le rhume**
Fever	**Une fièvre**
Hurt	**Se blesser**
Indigestion	**Une Indigestion**
Injury	**Une blessure**
Pain	**Une douleur**
Pulse	**Impulsion**
Sick	**Malade**
Sneeze	**Éternuement**
Sore throat	**Mal de gorge**
Toothache	**Mal aux dents**
I have a headache	**J'ai un mal de tête**
I have a stomachache	**J'ai mal à l'estomac**
I have pain in my knee	**J'ai mal au genou.**
I hurt my hand	**Je me suis blessé la main**
I've got a cold	**J'ai pris froid**
My foot hurts	**J'ai mal au pied**

50. The Animals
/ Les Animaux

Bear	**L'ours**
Bird	**L'oiseau**
Cat	**Le chat**
Chicken	**Le poulet**
Cow	**La vache**
Dog	**Le chien**
Duck	**Le canard**
Elephant	**L'éléphant**
Fish	**Le poisson**
Horse	**Le cheval**
Lizard	**Le lézard**
Lion	**Le lion**
Monkey	**Le singe**
Mouse	**La souris**
Rat	**Le rat**
Tiger	**Le tigre**

EXERCISE!

Write the French translation.

Keep practicing at:
QuickLanguages.com

1. Greetings
/ Les Salutations

Hi! / Hello!	Salut!
Good morning	
Good afternoon	
Good evening / Good night	
How are you doing?	
Fine	
Very well	
Thank you / Thanks	
Thank you very much	
You're welcome	
Fine, thank you	
And you?	
See you	
See you later	
See you tomorrow	
Goodbye	
Bye	

2. Introductions and Courtesy Expressions / **Les Présentations et Expressions de Politesse**

What is your name?	*Comment vous appelez-vous?*
My name is …	
Who are you?	
I am …	
Who is he / she?	
He is … / She is …	
Nice to meet you / Pleased to meet you	
Nice to meet you, too	
It's my pleasure	
Excuse me	
Please	
One moment, please	
Welcome	
Go ahead	
Can you repeat, please?	
I don't understand	
I understand a little	
Can you speak more slowly, please?	
Do you speak Spanish?	
How do you say hello in Spanish?	
What does it mean?	
I speak Spanish a little	

3. Ways to Address a Person
/ Formes de Désignation de la Personne

Madam / Ma'am	Madame
Miss	
Ms.	
Mr.	
Mrs.	
Sir	
Dr.	

4. The Articles
/ Les Articles

The	Le / la / les
The car	
The cars	
The house	
The houses	
A	
A car	
A house	
An	
An elephant	
An apple	
Some	
Some cars	
Some houses	

5. The Subject Pronouns
/ Les Pronoms Personnels

I	Je
You	
He	
She	
It	
We	
You	
They	

6. The Possessive Adjectives
/ Les Adjectifs Possessifs

My	Mon
Your	
His	
Her	
Its	
Our	
Your	
Their	
My car	
Your book	
His TV	
Our house	

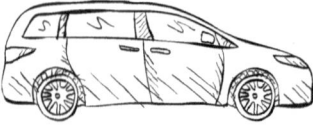

7. The Demonstrative Adjectives / **Les Adjectifs Démonstratifs**

This	Ce / Cette
This book	
This shirt	
These	
These books	
These shirts	
That	
That table	
That car	
Those	
Those tables	
Those cars	

8. The Possessive Pronouns / **Les Pronoms Possessifs**

Mine	Le mien
Yours	
His	
Hers	
Its	
Ours	
Yours	
Theirs	
The car is mine	
The book is yours	
That TV is his	
This house is ours	

9. The Cardinal Numbers
/ Les Nombres Cardinaux

0 / Zero	Zéro
1 / One	
2 / Two	
3 / Three	
4 / Four	
5 / Five	
6 / Six	
7 / Seven	
8 / Eight	
9 / Nine	
10 / Ten	
11 / Eleven	
12 / Twelve	
13 / Thirteen	
14 / Fourteen	
15 / Fifteen	
16 / Sixteen	
17 / Seventeen	
18 / Eighteen	
19 / Nineteen	
20 / Twenty	
21 / Twenty-one	
30 / Thirty	
40 / Forty	
50 / Fifty	
60 / Sixty	

1. 2. 3. 4.
5. 6. 7. 8.
9. 0.

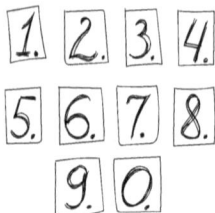

9. The Cardinal Numbers
/ Les Nombres Cardinaux

70 / Seventy	Soixante-dix
80 / Eighty	
90 /Ninety	
100 / One hundred	
101 / One hundred and one	
200 / Two hundred	
300 / Three hundred	
400 / Four hundred	
500 / Five hundred	
600 / Six hundred	
700 / Seven hundred	
800 / Eight hundred	
900 /Nine hundred	
1,000 / One thousand	
10,000 / Ten thousand	
100,000 / One hundred thousand	
1,000,000 / One million	
1,000,000,000 / One billion	
Forty-five (45)	
One hundred and twenty-eight (128)	
One thousand nine hundred and sixty-three (1,963)	
Six thousand and thirty-seven (6,037)	
Eleven thousand (11,000)	
Two hundred and seventy-nine thousand (279,000)	
Two million (2,000,000)	

10. The Time
/ L'heure

The clock

L'horloge

The watch

What time is it?

It is ...

It is one o'clock (1:00)

It is two o'clock (2:00)

It is three fifteen / It is a quarter past three (3:15)

It is four thirty / It is half past four (4:30)

It is five forty-five / It is a quarter to six (5:45)

It is six fifty / It is ten to seven (6:50)

It is noon (12:00 P. M.)

It is midnight (12:00 A. M.)

In the morning

In the afternoon

In the evening

At night

At what time is ...?

At what time is the concert?

At ...

At 7:10 P.M. (seven ten in the evening)

11. The Days of the Week
/ Les Jours de la Semaine

Monday	Lundi
Tuesday	
Wednesday	
Thursday	
Friday	
Saturday	
Sunday	
What day is today?	

12. The Months of the Year
/ Les Mois de l'année

January	Janvier
February	
March	
April	
May	
June	
July	
August	
September	
October	
November	
December	
What is today's date?	

13. The Weather
/ Le Temps

Sunny	Ensoleillé
Cloudy	
Rainy	
Humid	
Dry	
Cold	
Warm	
Hot	
Rain	
Snow	
How is the weather today?	
It's nice	
It's sunny	
It's cold in winter	
It's raining	
It's snowing	
I am cold	

14. The Seasons
/ Les Saisons

Spring	Printemps
Summer	
Fall	
Winter	

15. The Colors
/ Les Couleurs

Yellow	Jaune
Red	
Blue	
Green	
Orange	
Brown	
Pink	
Purple	
Black	
White	
Gray	
Light	
Dark	
Light green	
Orange book	
Brown shoes	
My blouse is white	
What color is...?	
What is your favorite color?	

16. The Parts of the Face
/ Les Parties du Visage(s)

La joue

Cheek	
Chin	
Ear	
Eye	
Forehead	
Hair	
Lips	
Mouth	
Nose	
Skin	
Teeth	
Tooth	
Blond / Blonde	
Brown	
Gray	
Red hair	
Long	
Short	
Straight	
Curly	
John is blond	
Karen has long hair	
He has green eyes	
Her eyes are blue	
His eyes are big and brown	

17. Essential Verbs
/ Verbes de Base

Be	Être
Go	
Come	
Have	
Get	
Help	
Love	
Like	
Want	
Buy	
Sell	
Read	
Write	
Drink	
Eat	
Open	
Close	
Look at	
Look for	
Find	
Start	
Stop	
Pull	

17. Essential Verbs
/ Verbes de Base

Push   *Pousser*

Send

Receive

Turn on

Turn off

Listen to

Speak

Do

Drive

Feel

Know

Leave

Live

Make

Meet

Need

Pay

Play

Remember

Repeat

Say

Sit

Sleep

17. Essential Verbs
/ Verbes de Base

Study	Étudier
Take	
Think	
Understand	
Wait	
Watch	
There is	
There are	
I am tall	
You are short	
He is thin	
We are big	
They are intelligent	
I am at home	
You are at school	
We are at the store	
I get a prize	
I go to the movies	
I have a nice car	
I listen to the music	
I watch TV.	
I like this book	
There are ten children in the park	

18. Interrogative Words
/ Les Adverbes Interrogatifs

How many ...?	Combien...?
How much...?	
How ...?	
What ...?	
When ...?	
Where ...?	
Which ...?	
Who ...?	
Whose ...?	
Whom ...? / To whom ...?	
Why ...?	
Because ...	

19. Linking Words
/ Les Conjonctions

And	Et
But	
Or	
Either ... or	
Neither ... nor	
Yes	
No	
So	
While	

20. The Prepositions
/ Les Prépositions

About	Concernant
Above	
Across	
At	
Behind	
Below	
Between	
By	
Down	
During	
For	
From	
In	
In front of	
Into	

20. The Prepositions
/ Les Prépositions

Near	Près de
Next to	
Of	
On	
Out	
Over	
Per	
Through	
To	
Under	
Up	
With	
Without	
The cat is in the box	
The vase is on the table	
Somebody is at the door	

21. Giving Directions
/ Les Indications

At the corner	Au coin
Far	
Near	
Go straight ahead	
Left	
Right	
Turn left	
Turn right	
Go straight one block	
After the traffic light, turn right	
How can I get to ...?	
Where is the ...?	
Where is the church?	
The museum is next to the shopping center	
The drugstore is in front of the building	
The supermarket is near the park	

22. The Ordinal Numbers
/ Les Nombres Ordinaux

English	French
First	Premier
Second	
Third	
Fourth	
Fifth	
Sixth	
Seventh	
Eighth	
Ninth	
Tenth	
Eleventh	
Twelfth	
Twentieth	
Thirtieth	
The first building	
The second floor	

23. Countries, Nationalities, and Languages / **Les Pays, Nationalités, et Langues**

Brazil (Country)	Le Brésil (Pays)
Brazilian (Nationality)	
Portuguese (Language)	
Colombia	
Colombian	
Spanish	
China	
Chinese	
Chinese	
England	
English	
English	
France	
French	
French	
Germany	
German	
German	
Italy	

23. Countries, Nationalities, and Languages / **Les Pays, Nationalités, et Langues**

Italian	Italien / Italienne
Italian	
Japan	
Japanese	
Japanese	
Mexico	
Mexican	
Spanish	
Spain	
Spanish	
Spanish	
United States of America (U.S.A.)	
American	
English	
Where are you from?	
I am from Brazil	
I am Brazilian	
I speak Portuguese	
I am not from Italy	

24. Indefinite Pronouns / Les Pronoms Indéfinis

Anybody	*Quelqu'un (interrogatif), personne (négatif)*
Anything	
Nobody	
Nothing	
Somebody	
Something	
Everybody	
Everything	
Is anybody home?	
I don't want anything	
Nothing happened	
Somebody is in the living room	
Everything is ready	

25. The Emotions
/ Les Émotions

Fâché, furieux

Angry	
Bored	
Confident	
Confused	
Embarrassed	
Excited	
Happy	
Nervous	
Proud	
Sad	
Scared	
Shy	
Surprised	
Worried	
I am happy	
He is sad	
They are surprised	
Are you excited?	
I am not bored	
She is not nervous	
Everybody is confident	

26. Adverbs
/ Les Adverbes

English	French
A few	Quelques
A little	
A lot	
After	
Again	
Ago	
Also	
Always	
Before	
Enough	
Everyday	
Exactly	
Finally	
First	
Here	
Late	
Later	
Never	
Next	
Now	

26. Adverbs
/ Les Adverbes

Often	Souvent
Once	
Only	
Outside	
Really	
Right here	
Right now	
Since	
Slowly	
Sometimes	
Soon	
Still	
Then	
There	
Today	
Tomorrow	
Tonight	
Too	
Usually	

27. Auxiliary Verbs
/ Autres Verbes

Pouvoir (possibilité)

Can

Could

Did

Do

Does

Have to

May

Must

Should

Will

Would

Can you go to the movies?

Could I have change?

Did you work at the drugstore?

I did not (didn't) work at the drugstore

Do you work at the drugstore?

I do not (don't) work at the drugstore

Does he read the newspaper?

He does not (doesn't) read the newspaper

I have to do my homework

May I help you?

You must turn left now

You should go to the doctor

I will work tomorrow

I would like a glass of wine

28. Expressions
/ Des Expressions

D'accord

All right
Come in
Come here, please
Don't worry!
For example
Good luck!
Great idea!
Have a nice day!
Help yourself!
Here you are
Hurry up!
I agree
I disagree
I don't care
I don't know
I'm coming!
I'm afraid...
It's a deal!
Keep well!
Let me think
Let's go!
Right now
Sounds good!
Sure
Take a seat
Take care!

29. The Family
/ La Famille

English	French
Father	Le père
Mother	
Son	
Daughter	
Brother	
Sister	
Grandfather	
Grandmother	
Uncle	
Aunt	
Cousin	
Nephew	
Niece	
Husband	
Wife	
Boyfriend	
Girlfriend	
In-laws	
Father in-law	
Mother in-law	
Brother in-law	
Sister in-law	
Step father	
Step mother	
Step brother	
Step sister	
Who is he?	
He is my brother	

30. The House
/ La Maison

Le salon

Living room

Door

Window

Sofa

Lamp

Dining room

Table

Chair

Kitchen

Stove

Oven

Fridge

Microwave

Bedroom

Bed

Nightstand

Vanity

Chest of drawers

Closet

Bathroom

Mirror

Sink

Toilet

Bathtub

Laundry room

Driveway

Where is the living room?

The door is big

The stove is small

The kitchen is beautiful

31. The City
/ La Ville

Block	Le paté de maison
Building	
Church	
Movie theater	
Museum	
Park	
Drugstore	
Restaurant	
Shopping center	
Store	
Street	
Supermarket	

32. At the Supermarket
/ Au Supermarché

La nourriture

The food	
The fruits	
Apple	
Banana	
Cherry	
Grapes	
Orange	
Strawberry	
The vegetables	
Beans	
Carrot	
Cauliflower	
Lettuce	
Onion	
Pepper	
Potato	
Tomato	
The meats	
Beef	
Chicken	
Turkey	
Ham	
Pork	
The dairy products	
Butter	
Cheese	
Milk	

32. At the Supermarket
/ Au Supermarché

Yogurt	Le yaourt
Jam	
Bread	
Eggs	
Fish	
Seafood	
Can	
Cart	
Bag	
Basket	
Bottle	
Cash register	
Cashier	
Customer service	
Groceries	
How many...?	
How many oranges do you buy?	
How much does it cost?	
How much do the bananas cost?	
I want...	
I want to buy a bottle of milk	
I would like...	
I would like a bag of tomatoes	
Where is the lettuce?	
It's on aisle one	
Where are the cans of vegetables?	
They are on aisle five	

33. At the Restaurant
/ Au Restaurant

Waiter / waitress	Le serveur / la serveuse
Breakfast	
Lunch	
Dinner	
To eat	
To drink	
To eat breakfast	
The menu	
Appetizer	
Salad	
Soup	
Main course	
Pasta	
Rice	
French fries	
Mashed potatoes	
Baked potatoes	
Barbecue	
Fried chicken	
Steak	

33. At the Restaurant
/ Au Restaurant

Dessert	Le dessert
Beverages	
Coffee	
Tea	
Soda	
Lemonade	
Orange juice	
Alcoholic drinks	
Beer	
Wine	
Check	
Tip	
How may I help you?	
What would you like to order?	
May I have the menu, please?	
Could I get more water, please?	
My order is wrong	
The service here is wonderful!	
The food is delicious!	
The check, please	
The tip is included	

34. The Office
/ Le Bureau

Book   *Le livre*

Calculator

Computer

Desk

Fax machine

File

File cabinet

Folder

Keyboard

Monitor

Mouse

Notebook

Pad

Paper

Pen

Printer

Ruler

Scissors

Screen

Stapler

Telephone

My computer is broken

There is no paper in the printer

We need to buy more folders

We don't have a copy machine

35. Jobs and Positions
/ Les Emplois et Positions

Accountant	Comptable
Architect	
Artist	
Chef	
Clerk	
Cook	
Doctor	
Engineer	
Gardener	
Graphic designer	
Lawyer	
Nurse	
Physician	
Salesperson	
Secretary	
Security guard	
Taxi driver	
Teacher	
Technician	
Tourist guide	
Travel agent	

36. Job Interview
/ Entretien Professionnel

Apply for a job	Postuler pour un poste
Duty	
Experience	
Last name	
First name	
Full time job	
Part time job	
Résumé	
Skill	
Work	

37. The Transportation
/ Les Moyens de Transport

Airplane	L'Avion
Bicycle	
Bus	
Car	
Helicopter	
Metro	
Motorcycle	
Train	
Truck	

38. The Traffic
/ La Circulation

English	French
Bus stop	La station de bus
Crosswalk	
Freeway, highway	
Gas station	
Intersection	
Lane	
No outlet	
One way	
Pedestrian	
Speed	
Stop sign	
To get in	
To get off	
Toll	
Traffic light	
Train station	
Two way	
U-turn	
Yield	
I get in the car	
I get off the car	
We wait for the train	

39. The Car
/ La Voiture

Accelerator	L'accélérateur
Battery	
Hood	
Brake	
Clutch	
Engine	
Fender	
Gear box	
Headlight	
Rear view mirror	
Make	
Model	
Radiator	
Steering wheel	
Seat	
Tire	
Trunk	
Wheel	
Windshield	
Windshield wipers	
The car is broken	
I have a flat tire	
I need a new battery	
What year is the car?	
What make is the car?	
What model is the car?	
How many miles does the car have?	

40. Phone Conversations / Des Conversations Téléphoniques

Call	Téléphoner
Dial	
Directory	
Directory Assistance	
Extension	
Hold on, please	
I'd like to speak to...	
I'll put you through	
I'll transfer your call	
I'm calling about ...	
Just a minute	
Leave a message	
Let me see...	
Phone	
Phone number	
Ring	
Speak	
Speaking	
Take a message	
Talk	
This is...	
Who's calling?	

41. At the Post Office
/ A la Poste

Air mail   *Par avion*

Counter

Envelope

Letter

Mail

Parcel

Postcard

Postman, mailman

Stamp

To send

To deliver

Delivery

To pick up

Address

I want to send a letter

I would like to pick up a parcel

How much do the stamps cost?

Do you sell postcards?

42. At the Bank
/ A la Banque

Account	Le compte
ATM	
Bank statement	
Bank teller	
Cash	
Checkbook	
Checking account	
Credit card	
Debit card	
Deposit slip	
Savings account	
To deposit	
To save	
To transfer	
To withdraw	
Transactions	
Withdrawal slip	
I want to make a deposit	
Do you have a savings account?	
I have a checking account	
What is your credit card number?	
I don't have an ATM card	
Where are the deposit slips?	

43. At the Airport
/ A l'Aéroport

Arrival — *Arrivée*

Concourse

Customs

Departure

Destination

Entrance

Exit

First class

Flight

Gate

Immigrations office

Luggage

Passport

Restrooms

Suitcase

To arrive

To depart

To travel

Trip

Where are you traveling?

May I have your ticket, please?

I need you passport, please

My flight number is ...

Where is gate number ...?

The flight is delayed

The flight is on time

44. At the Hotel
/ A l'Hôtel

English	French
Double room	La chambre double
Single room	
Bell desk	
Bellman	
Elevator	
Reception	
Receptionist	
Reservation	
Stairway	
Swimming pool	
Tours desk	
Valet parking	
To check-in	
To check-out	
I would like to make a reservation	
I want a single room	
I would like to check-in	

45. The Clothes
/ Les Vêtements

English	French
Bathing suit	Le maillot de bain
Belt	
Blouse	
Coat	
Dress	
Gloves	
Hat	
Jacket	
Pants	
Purse	
Scarf	
Shirt	
Shoes	
Shorts	
Skirt	
Socks	
Suit	
Suitcase	
The size	
Small	
Medium	
Large	
Big sizes	

46. At the Shopping Center
/ Au Centre Commercial

Department store	Département
Ladies	
Men	
Juniors	
Kids	
Ladies' department	
Jewelry	
Fitting room	
Elevator	
Escalator	
How may I help you?	
I'm looking for ...	
I'm just looking	
Where is the fitting room?	
It fits well	
It doesn't fit well	
May I pay here?	
I want to exchange this	
I want to return this	
I like ...	
I like this blouse	
I don't like ...	
I don't like these pants	

47. At the Drugstore
/ A la Pharmacie

Antiseptic   Le désinfectant

Adhesive bandage

Antibiotic

Aspirin

Bandage

Cold medicine

Cough syrup

Medication

Ointment

OTC (Over The Counter)
medication

Painkiller

Pills

Prescription

Tablets

Thermometer

Cotton

48. The Parts of the Body
/ Les Parties du Corps

Ankle	La cheville
Arm	
Back	
Buttock	
Calf	
Chest	
Elbow	
Feet	
Finger	
Foot	
Forearm	
Hand	
Head	
Hip	
Knee	
Leg	
Neck	
Shoulder	
Stomach	
Thigh	
Toe	
Waist	
Wrist	

49. Health Problems
/ Les Problèmes de Santé

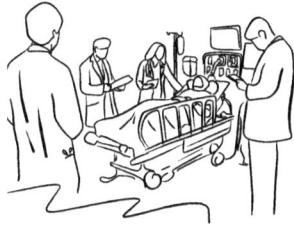

Backache	Douleurs dans le dos
Cold	
Fever	
Hurt	
Indigestion	
Injury	
Pain	
Pulse	
Sick	
Sneeze	
Sore throat	
Toothache	
I have a headache	
I have a stomachache	
I have pain in my knee	
I hurt my hand	
I've got a cold	
My foot hurts	

50. The Animals
/ Les Animaux

Bear	L'ours
Bird	
Cat	
Chicken	
Cow	
Dog	
Duck	
Elephant	
Fish	
Horse	
Lizard	
Lion	
Monkey	
Mouse	
Rat	
Tiger	

EXERCISE!

Write the English translation.

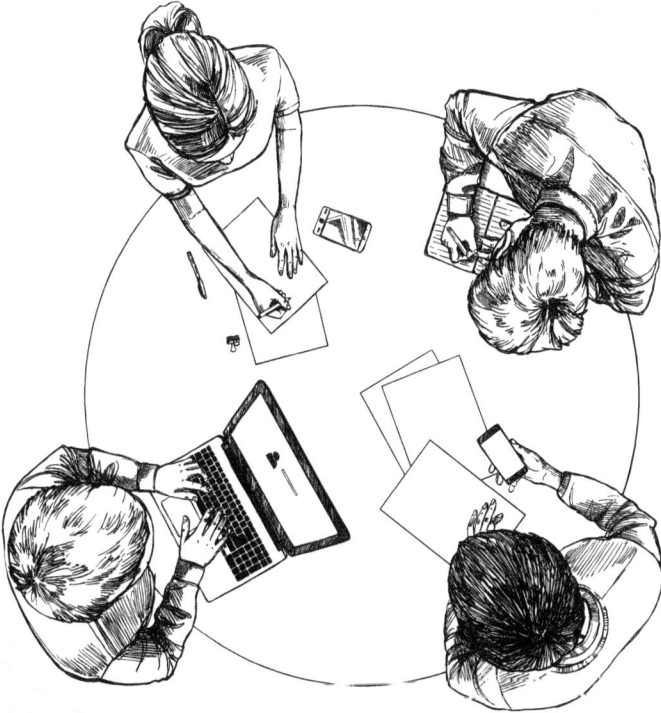

1. Greetings
/ Les Salutations

Salut!	Hi! / Hello!
Bonjour	
Bonjour	
Bonsoir/Bonne nuit	
Ça va?	
Bien	
Très bien	
Merci	
Merci beaucoup	
Pas de quoi	
Bien, merci	
Et toi?	
A bientôt!	
A plus tard!	
A demain!	
Au revoir!	
A plus!	

2. Introductions and Courtesy Expressions / **Les Présentations et Expressions de Politesse**

Comment vous appelez-vous?	What is your name?
Je m'appelle...	
Qui êtes-vous?	
Je suis...	
Qui est-il? / Qui est-elle?	
Il est .../ Elle est...	
Enchanté	
Moi aussi / Également	
C'est un plaisir	
Excusez-moi	
S'il vous plaît	
Un instant, s'il vous plaît	
Bienvenue	
Entrez, s'il vous plaît	
Pourriez-vous répéter, s'il vous plaît?	
Je ne comprends pas.	
Je comprends un petit peu.	
Pourriez-vous parler un peu plus lentement, s'il vous plaît?	
Parlez-vous espagnol?	
Comment dit-on "salut" en espagnol?	
Qu'est-ce que ça veut dire?	
Je parle un peu espagnol.	

3. Ways to Address a Person
/ Formes de Désignation de la Personne

Madame	Madam / Ma'am
Mademoiselle	
Mlle	
M	
Mme	
Monsieur	
Docteur	

4. The Articles
/ Les Articles

Le / la / les	The
La voiture	
Les voitures	
La maison	
Les maisons	
Un / une	
Une voiture	
Une maison	
Un / une	
Un éléphant	
Une pomme	
Des	
Des voitures	
Des maisons	

5. The Subject Pronouns
/ Les Pronoms Personnels

Je	I
Tu	
Il / On	
Elle	
∅	
Nous	
Vous	
Ils	

6. The Possessive Adjectives
/ Les Adjectifs Possessifs

Mon	My
Ton	
Son	
Sa	
Son	
Notre	
Votre	
Leur	
Ma voiture	
Ton livre	
Son téléviseur	
Notre maison	

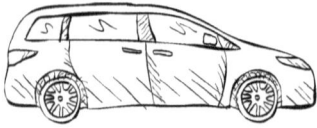

7. The Demonstrative Adjectives / **Les Adjectifs Démonstratifs**

Ce / Cette	This
Ce livre	
Cette chemise	
Ces	
Ces livres	
Ces chemises	
Ce / cette	
Cette table	
Cette voiture	
Ces	
Ces tables	
Ces voitures	

8. The Possessive Pronouns / **Les Pronoms Possessifs**

Le mien	Mine
Le tien	
Le sien	
La sienne	
Le sien	
Le nôtre	
Le vôtre	
Le leur	
La voiture est à moi	
Le livre est à toi	
Le téléviseur est à lui	
Cette maison est à nous	

9. The Cardinal Numbers
/ **Les Nombres Cardinaux**

Zéro	0 / Zero
Un	
Deux	
Trois	
Quatre	
Cinq	
Six	
Sept	
Huit	
Neuf	
Dix	
Onze	
Douze	
Treize	
Quatorze	
Quinze	
Seize	
Dix-sept	
Dix-huit	
Dix-neuf	
Vingt	
Vingt-et-un	
Trente	
Quarante	
Cinquante	
Soixante	

1. 2. 3. 4.
5. 6. 7. 8.
9. 0.

9. The Cardinal Numbers
/ Les Nombres Cardinaux

Soixante-dix	70 / Seventy
Quatre-vingt	
Quatre-vingt-dix	
Cent	
Cent un	
Deux cent	
Trois cent	
Quatre cent	
Cinq cent	
Six cent	
Sept cent	
Huit cent	
Neuf cent	
Mille	
Dix mille	
Cent mille	
Un million	
Un milliard	
Quarante cinq	
Cent vingt-huit	
Mille neuf cent soixante-trois	
Six mille trente-sept	
Onze mille	
Deux cent soixante-dix-neuf mille	
Deux millions	

10. The Time
/ L'heure

L'horloge

The clock

La montre

Quelle heure est-il?

Il est...

Il est une heure (1h00)

Il est deux heures (2h00)

Il est trois heures quinze / Il est trois heures et quart (3h15)

Il est quatre heures trente / Il est quatre heures et demi (4h30)

Il est cinq heures quarante cinq / Il est six heures moins quart (5h45)

Il est six heures cinquante / Il est sept heures moins dix (6h50)

Il est midi (12h00)

Il est minuit (00h00)

Le matin

L'après-midi

Le soir

La nuit

A quelle heure est....?

A quelle heure commence le concert?

A...

A 7:10 (sept heures dix du soir)

SUNDAY
MONDAY
TUESDAY
WEDNESDAY
THURSDAY
/FRIDAY
SATURDAY

11. The Days of the Week
/ Les Jours de la Semaine

Lundi	Monday
Mardi	
Mercredi	
Jeudi	
Vendredi	
Samedi	
Dimanche	
Quel jour sommes-nous?	

February June October
March July November
April August December
May September

12. The Months of the Year
/ Les Mois de l'année

Janvier	January
Février	
Mars	
Avril	
Mai	
Juin	
Juillet	
Août	
Septembre	
Octobre	
Novembre	
Décembre	
Quelle est la date d'aujourd'hui?	

13. The Weather
/ Le Temps

Ensoleillé	*Sunny*
Nuageux	
Pluvieux	
Humide	
Sec	
Froid	
Chaud	
Très chaud	
Pluie	
Neige	
Quel temps fait-il aujourd'hui?	
Il fait beau	
C'est ensoleillé.	
En hiver il fait froid	
Il pleut	
Il neige	
J'ai froid	

14. The Seasons / Les Saisons

Printemps	*Spring*
Été	
Automne	
Hiver	

15. The Colors / Les Couleurs

Jaune	*Yellow*
Rouge	
Bleu	
Vert	
Orange	
Marron	
Rose	
Violet	
Noir	
Blanc	
Gris	
Clair	
Foncé	
Vert clair	
Un livre orange	
Des chaussures marrons	
Ma blouse est blanche	
De quelle couleur est...?	
Quelle est ta couleur préférée?	

16. The Parts of the Face
/ Les Parties du Visage(s)

Cheek

La joue

Le menton

L'oreille

L'œil

Le front

Les cheveux

Les lèvres

La bouche

Le nez

La peau

Les dents

Le dent

Blond / Blonde

Brun

Cheveux gris

Roux

Long

Court

Raide

Frisé

John est blond

Karen a les cheveux longs

Il a les yeux verts

Ses yeux sont bleus

Ses yeux sont grands et marrons

17. Essential Verbs
/ Verbes de Base

Être	Be
Aller	
Venir	
Avoir	
Prendre / obtenir	
Aider	
Aimer	
Apprécier	
Vouloir	
Acheter	
Vendre	
Lire	
Écrire	
Boire	
Manger	
Ouvrir	
Fermer	
Regarder	
Chercher	
Trouver	
Commencer	
Arrêter	
Tirer	

17. Essential Verbs
/ Verbes de Base

Pousser	Push
Envoyer	
Recevoir	
Allumer	
Éteindre	
Écouter	
Parler	
Faire	
Conduire	
Sentir	
Savoir	
Partir / sortir	
Vivre	
Faire, effectuer, fabriquer	
Rencontrer	
Avoir besoin	
Payer	
Jouer	
Se rappeler	
Répéter	
Dire	
S'asseoir	
Dormir	

17. Essential Verbs
/ Verbes de Base

French	English
Étudier	Study
Prendre	
Penser	
Comprendre	
Attendre	
Regarder	
Il y a	
Il y a	
Je suis grand	
Tu es petit	
Il est maigre	
Nous sommes grands	
Ils sont intelligents	
Je suis à la maison	
Tu es à l'école	
Nous sommes au magasin	
Je reçois un prix	
Je vais au cinéma	
J'ai une belle voiture	
J'écoute la musique	
Je regarde la télévision	
J'aime bien ce livre	
Il y a dix enfants dans le parc	

18. Interrogative Words
/ Les Adverbes Interrogatifs

Combien...?	How many ...?
Combien...?	
Comment...?	
Quoi...?	
Quand...?	
Où...?	
Lequel...? / Laquelle...?	
Qui...?	
A qui...?	
A qui...?	
Pourquoi...?	
Parce que...?	

NO!

YES!

19. Linking Words
/ Les Conjonctions

Et	And
Mais	
Ou	
Ou bien ... ou ...	
Ni...ni...	
Oui	
Non	
Donc	
Pendant	

20. The Prepositions / Les Prépositions

Concernant	About
Au dessus	
A travers	
A, sur, vers	
Derrière	
Au dessous	
Entre	
Par	
En bas	
Durant	
Pour	
De	
Dans, en	
En face / devant	
En	

20. The Prepositions
/ Les Prépositions

Près de	*Near*
A côté	
De	
Sur / par dessus	
Dehors	
Sur	
Par	
A travers	
Vers	
Sous	
En haut	
Avec	
Sans	
Le chat est dans la boîte	
Le vase est sur la table	
Quelqu'un est à la porte	

21. Giving Directions
/ Les Indications

Au coin	At the corner
Loin	
Proche	
Continuez tout droit	
A gauche	
A droite	
Tournez à gauche	
Tournez à droite	
Continuez tout droit, sur un pâte de maison	
Après le feu, tournez à droite	
Comment puis-j'aller à ...?	
Où se trouve...?	
Où se trouve l'église?	
Le musée se trouve à côté du centre commercial	
La pharmacie se trouve en face du bâtiment	
Le supermarché est près du parc	

22. The Ordinal Numbers
/ Les Nombres Ordinaux

Premier	First
Deuxième	
Troisième	
Quatrième	
Cinquième	
Sixième	
Septième	
Huitième	
Neuvième	
Dixième	
Onzième	
Douzième	
Vingtième	
Trentième	
Le premier bâtiment	
Le deuxième étage	

23. Countries, Nationalities, and Languages / **Les Pays, Nationalités, et Langues**

Le Brésil (Pays)	Brazil (Country)
brésilien, brésilienne (Nationalité)	
Portugais (Langue)	
La Colombie	
Colombien / Colombienne	
Espagnol	
La Chine	
Chinois / Chinoise	
Chinois	
L'Angleterre	
Anglais / Anglaise	
Anglais	
La France	
Français / Française	
Français	
L'Allemagne	
Allemand / Allemande	
Allemand	
L'Italie	

23. Countries, Nationalities, and Languages / **Les Pays, Nationalités, et Langues**

Italien / Italienne   Italian

Italien

Le Japon

Japonais / Japonaise

Japonais

Le Mexique

Mexicain / Mexicaine

Espagnol

L'Espagne

Espagnol / Espagnole

Espagnol

Les États Unis d'Amérique

Américain / Américaine

Anglais

D'où êtes vous?

Je suis du Brésil

Je suis brésilien

Je parle portugais

Je ne suis pas d'Italie

24. Indefinite Pronouns
/ Les Pronoms Indéfinis

Quelqu'un (interrogatif), personne (négatif)	Anybody
Quelque chose (interrogatif), rien (négatif)	
Personne	
Rien	
Quelqu'un (affirmatif)	
Quelque chose (affirmatif)	
Tous	
Tout	
Y a-t-il quelqu'un dans la maison?	
Je ne veux rien	
Il ne s'est rien passé	
Quelqu'un est dans le salon	
Tout est prêt	

25. The Emotions
/ Les Émotions

Angry

Fâché, furieux

Ennuyeux

Sûr de soi

Confondu

Embarrassé

Enthousiaste

Heureux

Nerveux

Fier

Triste

Effrayé

Timide

Surpris

Soucieux

Je suis heureux

Il est triste

Ils sont surpris

Es-tu enthousiaste?

Je ne m'ennuie pas

Elle n'est pas nerveuse

Ils sont tous sûrs d'eux

26. Adverbs
/ Les Adverbes

Quelques	A few
Peu	
Beaucoup	
Après	
Encore	
Avant	
Aussi	
Toujours	
Il y a	
Suffisant	
Chaque jour	
Exactement	
En fin de compte / Finalement	
D'abord	
Ici	
Tard	
Plus tard	
Jamais	
Suivant	
Maintenant	

26. Adverbs
/ Les Adverbes

Souvent	Often
Une fois	
Seulement	
Dehors	
Vraiment	
Ici	
Tout de suite	
Depuis	
Lentement	
Puisque	
Bientôt	
Toujours	
Plus tard	
Là-bas	
Aujourd'hui	
Demain	
Ce soir	
Aussi	
Habituellement / Normalement	

27. Auxiliary Verbs
/ Autres Verbes

Pouvoir (possibilité)	*Can*
Pouvoir (amabilité)	
Être / Avoir (pour la formation des temps composés)	
Faire	
Faire	
Il faut + infinitif	
Pouvoir (pour demander la permission)	
Devoir (obligation)	
Devoir (pour conseiller)	
(Auxiliare du Temps Futur)	
(Auxiliare du Conditionel)	
Peux-tu venir au cinéma?	
Pourrais-je avoir de la monnaie?	
Tu as travaillé à la pharmacie?	
Je n'ai pas travaille à la pharmacie?	
Est-ce que tu travailles à la pharmacie	
Je ne travaille pas à la pharmacie	
Est-ce qu'il lit le journal?	
Il ne lit pas le journal	
Je dois faire mon devoir	
Est-ce que je peux t'aider?	
Tu dois tourner à gauche	
Tu devrais aller chez le docteur	
Demain je travaillerai	
J'aimerais un verre de vin	

28. Expressions
/ Des Expressions

D'accord — All right

Entre / Entrez

Venez ici, s'il vous plaît

Ne t'inquiète pas!

Par exemple

Bon courage!

Excellente idée!

Bonne journée!

Sers-toi!

S'il vous plaît!

Dépêche-toi!

Je suis d'accord

Je ne suis pas d'accord

Ça ne m'intéresse pas

Je ne sais pas

Je viens

J'ai bien peur que...

Marché conclu!

Prends soin de toi!!

Laisse-moi réfléchir

Allons-y!

Tout de suite!

Ça me paraît bien

Sûrement

Assieds-toi / Asseyez-vous!

Prends soin de toi!

29. The Family
/ La Famille

French	English
Le père	*Father*
La mère	
Le fils	
La fille	
Le frère	
Le sœur	
Le grand-père	
La grand-mère	
L'oncle	
La tante	
Le cousin / la cousine	
Le neveu	
La nièce	
Le mari	
La femme	
Le fiancé	
La fiancée	
Les beaux-parents	
Le beau-père	
La belle-mère	
Le beau-frère	
La belle-soeur	
Le beau-père	
La belle-mère	
Le demi-frère	
La demi-soeur	
Qui est-il?	
C'est mon frère	

30. The House
/ La Maison

Living room

Le salon

La porte

La fenêtre

Le canapé

La lampe

La salle à manger

La table

La chaise

La cuisine

La cuisinière

Le four

Le réfrigérateur

Le four à micro-ondes

La chambre à coucher

Le lit

La table de nuit

La coiffeuse

La commode

Le vestiaire

La salle de bain

Le miroir

Le lavabo

Les toilettes

La baignoire

La chambre d'utilité

Le parking

Où se trouve le salon?

La porte est grande

La cuisinière est petite

La cuisine est belle

31. The City
/ La Ville

Le paté de maison	Block
L'immeuble	
L'église	
Le cinéma	
Le musée	
Le parc	
La pharmacie	
Le restaurant	
Le centre commercial	
Le magasin	
La rue	
Le supermarché	

32. At the Supermarket
/ Au Supermarché

La nourriture — The food

Les fruits

La pomme

La banane

La cerise

Les raisins

L'orange

La fraise

Les légumes

Les haricots

La carotte

Le chou-fleur

La laitue

L'oignon

Le poivron

La pomme de terre / la patate

La tomate

Les viandes

Le boeuf

Le poulet

La dinde

Le jambon

Du porc

Les produits laitiers

Le beurre

Le fromage

Le lait

32. At the Supermarket
/ Au Supermarché

Le yaourt	Yogurt
La confiture	
Le pain	
Les œufs	
Le poisson	
Les fruits de mer	
La conserve	
Le caddie	
Le sac	
Le panier	
La bouteille	
La caisse	
Le caissier / la caissière	
Le service aux clients	
Épicerie	
Combien...?	
Combien d'oranges achetez-vous...?	
Combien coûte ...? / Combien coûtent ... ?	
Combien coûtent les bananes?	
Je veux...	
Je veux acheter une bouteille de lait	
J'aimerais ...	
Je voudrais un sac de tomates	
Où sont les laitues?	
Elles sont dans l'allée numéro un	
Où se trouvent les conserves de légumes?	
Ils sont dans l'allée numéro cinq	

33. At the Restaurant
/ Au Restaurant

Le serveur / la serveuse	Waiter / waitress
Petit-déjeuner	
Déjeuner	
Dîner	
Manger	
Boire	
Prendre le petit-déjeuner	
Le menu	
L'entrée	
La salade	
La soupe	
Le repas principal	
Les pates	
Le riz	
Les frites	
La purée de pomme de terre	
Patates au four	
Le barbecue	
Du poulet roti	
Le bifteck	

33. At the Restaurant
/ **Au Restaurant**

Le dessert	Dessert
Les boissons	
Le café	
Le thé	
La boisson gazeuse	
Le limonade	
Le jus d'orange	
Les boissons alcoolisées	
La bière	
Le vin	
L'addition	
Le pourboire	
Que désirez-vous?	
Qu'allez-vous commander?	
Le menu, s'il vous plaît!	
Pourriez-vous m'apporter encore un peu plus d'eau, s'il vous plaît?	
Je n'ai pas commandé ça	
Le service est très bon ici	
La nourriture est délicieuse	
L'addition, s'il vous plaît	
Le pourboire est inclus	

34. The Office
/ Le Bureau

Le livre	Book
La calculatrice	
L'ordinateur	
Le bureau	
Le fax	
Le fichier	
Le classeur	
La chemise	
Le clavier	
Le moniteur	
La souris	
L'agenda	
Le bloc-notes	
Le papier	
Le stylo	
L'imprimante	
La règle	
Les ciseaux	
L'écran	
L'agrafeuse	
Le téléphone	
Mon ordinateur est cassé	
Il n'y a pas de papier dans l'imprimante	
Nous devons acheter encore des chemises	
Nous n'avons pas de photocopieuse	

35. Jobs and Positions
/ Les Emplois et Positions

Comptable	*Accountant*
Architecte	
Artiste	
Cuisinier en chef	
Un employé de bureau / une employée de bureau	
Cuisinier / cuisinière	
Docteur	
Ingénieur	
Jardinier	
Graphiste	
Avocat	
Infirmier / Infirmière	
Médecin	
Vendeur / Vendeuse	
Secrétaire	
Gardien	
Chauffeur de taxi	
Professeur	
Technicien	
Guide touristique	
Agent de voyage	

36. Job Interview
/ Entretien Professionnel

Postuler pour un poste　　　Apply for a job

En poste

Expérience

Nom de famille

Prénom

Travail à temps plein

Travail à temps partiel

Curriculum Vitae

Compétences

Travailler / Travail

37. The Transportation
/ Les Moyens de Transport

L'Avion　　　Airplane

Le vélo

L'autobus

La voiture

L' hélicoptère

Le métro

La moto

Le train

Le camion

38. The Traffic
/ La Circulation

French	English
La station de bus	Bus stop
Le passage piéton	
L'autoroute	
La station d'essence	
Le carrefour	
La file	
La rue sans issue	
La rue à sens unique	
Le piéton	
La vitesse	
Le signe "Stop"	
Monter / Rentrer dans	
Descendre de / Sortir de	
Le péage	
Le feu rouge	
La gare ferroviaire	
Aller-retour	
Demi-tour	
Accorder la priorité à	
Je rentre dans la voiture	
Je descends de la voiture	
Nous attendons le train	

39. The Car
/ La Voiture

L'accélérateur — Accelerator

La batterie

Le capot

Le frein

L'embrayage

Le moteur

L'aile

La boîte de vitesse

Les phares

Le rétroviseur

La marque

Le model

Le radiateur

Le volant

Le siège

Le pneu

Le coffre

La roue

Le pare-brise

Essuie-glace

La voiture est en panne

J'ai une creveson

J'ai besoin d'une nouvelle batterie

De quelle année est la voiture?

Quelle est la marque de la voiture?

Quel est le model de la voiture?

Combien de milles a la voiture?

40. Phone Conversations / Des Conversations Téléphoniques

Téléphoner	Call
Composer un numéro	
Annuaire téléphonique	
Les renseignements	
Numéro interne	
Ne raccrochez pas, s'il vous plaît / Un instant s'il vous plaît	
J'aimerais parler avec...	
Je vous passe...	
Je vous transfert la conversation	
Je vous téléphone concernant...	
Attendez une minute	
Laisser un message	
Laissez-moi regarder	
Téléphoner	
Numéro de téléphone	
Sonner	
Parler	
Au téléphone	
Transmettre quelque chose	
Parler	
C'est ... à l'appareil	
Qui est à l'appareil?	

41. At the Post Office
/ A la Poste

Par avion	Air mail
Guichet	
L'enveloppe	
La lettre	
Le courrier	
Le colis	
La carte postale	
Le facteur	
Le timbre	
Envoyer	
Livrer	
Livraison	
Prendre	
Adresse	
Je veux envoyer une lettre	
Je voudrais prendre un colis	
Quel est le prix des timbres?	
Est-ce que vous vendez des cartes postales?	

42. At the Bank
/ A la Banque

French	English
Le compte	Account
Le distributeur automatique	
Le relevé banquaire	
Le caissier / la caissière	
L'argent liquide	
Le chéquier	
Le compte chèque	
La carte de crédit	
La carte de débit	
La fiche de dépôt	
Le compte épargne	
Déposer	
Épargner	
Faire un transfert	
Retirer / Faire un retrait	
Les transactions	
Le reçu	
Je voudrais faire un dépôt	
Est-ce que vous avez un compte épargne?	
J'ai un compte courant.	
Quel est le numéro de votre carte de crédit?	
Je n'ai pas de carte de retrait.	
Où sont les fiches du dépôt?	

43. At the Airport
/ A l'Aéroport

Arrivée

Arrival

La salle d'attente

Les douanes

Départ

Destination

Entrée

Sortie

Première classe

Le vol

La porte

Le service d'immigration

Les bagages

Le passeport

Les toilettes

La valise

Arriver

Partir

Voyager

Voyage

Où allez-vous?

Puis-je voir votre billet, s'il vous plaît?

Montrez-moi votre passeport, s'il vous plaît

Le numéro de mon vol est le...

Où est la porte numéro...?

Le vol est en retard

Le vol est à l'heure

44. At the Hotel
/ A l'Hôtel

La chambre double	Double room
La chambre simple	
Le bureau d'information	
Le porteur	
L' ascenseur	
La réception	
Le/la réceptionniste	
La réservation	
L'escalier	
La piscine	
Le bureau du tourisme	
Le service de parking	
L'enregistrement	
L'enregistrement	
Je voudrais faire une réservation	
Je voudrais une chambre simple	
Je voudrais m'enregistrer	

45. The Clothes
/ Les Vêtements

Le maillot de bain	Bathing suit
La ceinture	
La blouse	
Le manteau	
La robe	
Les gants	
Le chapeau	
Le veston	
Les pantalons	
Le sac	
Le foulard	
La chemise	
Les chaussures	
Un short	
La jupe	
Les chaussettes	
Le costume	
La valise	
La taille	
Petite	
Moyenne	
Grande	
Grandes tailles	

46. At the Shopping Center / **Au Centre Commercial**

French	English
Département	Department store
Dames	
Messieurs	
Adolescents	
Enfants	
Départment des dames	
La bijouterie	
La cabine d'essayage	
L'ascenseur	
L'escalator	
Puis-je vous aider?	
Je cherche...	
Je ne fais que regarder	
Où est la cabine d'essayage?	
Ça me va bien?	
Ça ne me va pas bien	
Est-ce que je peux payer ici?	
Je voudrais changer cela	
Je voudrais rendre ça	
Ça me plaît	
Cette blouse me plaît	
Ça ne me plaît pas	
Ce pantalon ne me plaît pas	

47. At the Drugstore
/ A la Pharmacie

Le désinfectant — Antiseptic

L'adhésif

L'antibiotique

L'aspirine

La bande de pansement

Le médicament pour
refroidissement

Le sirop pour la toux

Les médicaments

La pommade

Les médicaments génériques

Le calmant

Les pastilles

La prescription

Les tablettes

Le thermomètre

Le coton

48. The Parts of the Body
/ Les Parties du Corps

La cheville	Ankle
Le bras	
Le dos	
Les fesses	
Le mollet	
La poitrine	
Le coude	
Les pieds	
Le doigt	
Le pied	
L'avant-bras	
La main	
La tête	
La hanche	
Le genou	
La jambe	
Le cou	
L'épaule	
L'estomac	
La cuisse	
L'orteil	
Le tour de taille	
Le poignet	

49. Health Problems
/ Les Problèmes de Santé

Douleurs dans le dos	Backache
Le rhume	
Une fièvre	
Se blesser	
Une Indigestion	
Une blessure	
Une douleur	
Impulsion	
Malade	
Éternuement	
Mal de gorge	
Mal aux dents	
J'ai un mal de tête	
J'ai mal à l'estomac	
J'ai mal au genou.	
Je me suis blessé la main	
J'ai pris froid	
J'ai mal au pied	

50. The Animals
/ Les Animaux

French	English
L'ours	Bear
L'oiseau	
Le chat	
Le poulet	
La vache	
Le chien	
Le canard	
L'éléphant	
Le poisson	
Le cheval	
Le lézard	
Le lion	
Le singe	
La souris	
Le rat	
Le tigre	

QUICK LANGUAGES

MULTI-LANGUAGE PHRASEBOOK COLLECTION

SPEAK ANY LANGUAGE NOW!

QUICK LANGUAGES PHRASEBOOK COLLECTION
AVAILABLE TITLES

1. ENGLISH-SPANISH & SPANISH-ENGLISH
2. ENGLISH-ITALIAN & ITALIAN-ENGLISH
3. ENGLISH-FRENCH & FRENCH-ENGLISH
4. ENGLISH-GERMAN & GERMAN-ENGLISH
5. ENGLISH-PORTUGUESE & PORTUGUESE-ENGLISH
6. ENGLISH-CHINESE & CHINESE-ENGLISH
7. ENGLISH-ARABIC & ARABIC-ENGLISH
8. ENGLISH-JAPANESE & JAPANESE-ENGLISH
9. ENGLISH-KOREAN & KOREAN-ENGLISH
10. ENGLISH-RUSSIAN & RUSSIAN-ENGLISH
11. ENGLISH-TURKISH & TURKISH-ENGLISH

GET THE AUDIOVISUAL AND INTERACTIVE CONTENT AT QuickLanguages.com

www.ingramcontent.com/pod-product-compliance
Lightning Source LLC
LaVergne TN
LVHW021452080426
835509LV00018B/2253